Leroy Shane

The Shepherd of the Sand Hills
and
The Life of the Party

Chris Miksanek

Laughter is the best medicine.
Amoxicillin is a close 2nd.

Acknowledgements

Here in *The Shepherd of the Sand Hills and The Life of the Party* I bounce around quite a bit from topic to topic and person to person in a seemingly herky-jerky style. In that way I am like the subject of this book himself who likewise darted like a Leaping Lena between opportunities making hay while the sun shined at the same time providing entertainment and inspiration to all who crossed his path.

But I was not alone in this effort. Numerous people shared their memories, materials or otherwise assisted including Mark Sobelman, Dick Sternberg, Brent Coggins, Ray Raver, Erika Austin, Charlie Pappas, Ken Zubay, Jeff Pieters, the St. Paul Pioneer Press, and the Mayo Clinic.

Table of Contents

Introduction

A popular destination on my 10-speed bike during my formative years was the iconic Chicago-area gag shop, Riley's Trick Shop (review: https://tinyurl.com/y2j47ww4). There could be procured all of the essentials necessary to satisfy a sophomoric wit like fake vomit and fake dog doo-doo, as well as standards like hand buzzers and whoopee cushions.

If Riley's was an influence in my burgeoning interest in comedy or if that interest was latent and I gravitated towards the south side shop to satisfy a visceral craving only therapy can determine but decades later, this interest in humor has not waned.

Since that time, for instance, I have attempted comedy writing with minor success and standup comedy with none. Then there is my comedy collection: scores of books, tapes and DVDs, some more than 100 years old, representing many of history's greatest comedic minds. Content from less familiar names like Milt Josefsberg and Larry Gelbart — both of whom I was fortunate enough to have met and who were generous with their time, their reminiscences, and, in some cases, with their comedic suggestions for a project — and from titans in the field like Jack Benny, Steve Allen, Bob Hope, and Milton Berle.

Ahhh, Milton Berle. A particular favorite of mine whom I met twice (unfortunately before the days of ubiquitous cell-phone cameras so you'll have to take my word).

It was in once such addition to my collection, a 1949 magazine of laughs with Berle on the cover, that I was introduced to arguably one of the most famous Minnesotans that I had never heard of: Leroy Shane.

Shane had been a fixture in the *Med City* since the 1940's, setting-up shop after determining the home to the Mayo Clinic could benefit from some levity — laughter being the best medicine and all. But his milieu was not limited to pranks and gifts, as you'll learn. He was essential to the town's development as an employer and his civic-mindedness and business acumen were instrumental in the early success of the Ability Building Community, which for decades has provided employment and vocational services for persons with disabilities and other special needs.

This intersection of humor and urban history piqued my curiosity, inspired a tangential collection, and this book.

It all started with a full-page ad in the aforementioned magazine for Shane's ***Fun of the Month Club***.

The Fun of the Month Club

The *Fun of the Month Club* holds a special place in my heart. An advertisement for it in a vintage joke magazine is where, of course, I was first introduced to Leroy Shane. The notion of such an operation — imagining the excitement of periodic fun surprises delivered to my mailbox — sent me back to childhood.

The original ad proclaimed:

Now! Fun for all.

It's fun for all and all for fun when you're a "Fun of the Month" club member.

Brothers and sisters, NOW is the time for you to join the newest, merriest, most laugh-getting club of all time! The FUN OF THE MONTH CLUB has been getting hundreds of new members every day from all over the country, and you don't want to miss out on all the gay gags and fun-makers that are coming your way every month.

The really amazing part of a FUN OF THE MONTH membership is this: these games and gimmicks are worth lots more than your membership price of $6.00 for six laugh-filled months or $11.00 for a full, rollicking year. You can't buy these gags at any old store, either, because most everything you get can be yours only through a FUN OF THE MONTH

The ad included several sidebars, one of which was this:

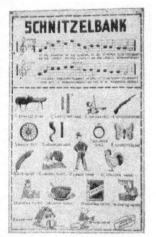

Here's the SCHNIT-ZELBANK… just one of the laugh-getters you'll be receiving… a riot of music and gaiety at any gathering!

membership! And only FUN OF THE MONTH can afford to send you these fun-makers at the lowest possible prices.

Becoming a member is just about the easiest thing in the world… all you do is fill out the coupon below, enclose your check, money order, or straight cash, and send it along to the Old Rib-Ticklers. Then you'll really start enjoying yourself! No more wondering what to do at parties, because you'll always have the latest games, the newest gags to spring on your friends. And you'll be winning new friends, too. Everybody loves to laugh and they love the people that made them laugh. You'll be the most popular party-giver in town… through a FUN OF THE MONTH CLUB membership!

THE OLD RIB-TICKLERS GUARANTEE: You're going to get loads of laughs from everything you receive or you'll get your money back!

The PARTY FUN APRON makes any party a real live affair… each pocket is filled with more laughs than a barrel of monkeys!

The ENCYCLOPEDIA WITTANICA and the FISHING PARTY SET are two more of the swell party games and surprise gags in store for you. Remember: whatever the game or gimmick may be, it's sure to keep you laughing until the next one comes along.

Membership in the *Fun of the Month Club* was only $6 for six months or $11 for a full year with various discounts available. Of course, $6 in 1948, accounting for inflation, would be about $66.50 today, perhaps out of the reach of a child though well within the reach of someone young at heart. Monthly trinkets ranged from joke business-card

Another sidebar promoted Shane's magic offerings:

FOR THE MAGIC-MINDED!

FUN OF THE MONTH'S "TRICK & MAGIC" MEMBERSHIP...

How would you like to receive a special kit each month containing 3 or 4 of the latest, most fascinating magic tricks? You can... through a FUN OF THE MONTH "Trick and Magic" membership. The fees are the same as a regular FUN OF THE MONTH membership. Send coupon today for full information to FUN OF THE MONTH'S "Trick and Magic Department"!

size notes on up, many of which are described in the section of this book discussing the Bar Boy Bib (page 44).

Shane and then-President Phil Sternberg evidently peppered the media of the time with press releases. Two of which got play in Shane's hometown newspaper *The Cincinnati Enquirer* in 1948. One read:

DAILY THOUGHT: Laugh and the world laughs with you; Weep, and you weep alone. This tad old earth must borrow its mirth. It has troubles enough of its own. Ella Wheeler Wilcox. 1883. Ha! *Fun of the Month Club.*

WELL, SIR, TODAY WE ARE as confused as a pair of strange skunks trapped in a cement mixer. We had thought, in our dumb and trusting way, that every possible kind of "Of The Month Club" had already been thought up. It started, you know, with a Book of the Month Club. Then it went from there to a Gift of the Month Club, then a Candy of the Month Club, then a

Flowers of the Month Club, and out in Hollywood we think they must have even had Husband Of The Month and Wife Of The Month Clubs. We thought it had reached the point where if you joined enough clubs you could just lay back and at least once every month everything conceivable would happen to you. There were only a couple of obscure possibilities that we thought they never would get around to. But now we don't even know about them.

YESTERDAY we opened the mail and these was an envelope full of stuff saying: "Live Laugh Be Merry!" Join the Fun of The Month Club!" Yes, Mr. Phil Sternberg, President, of Rochester, Minn., advised us that upon receipt of $3 he will send us postpaid, once a month for six months, an "Outstanding ADULT party fun item ... a little spicy, perhaps, but always clever always funny destined to be the life of the party." Mr. Sternberg said: "If you're looking for fun, we're looking for you." Hmm.

If we weren't a little pinched from Christmas shopping we would love to have this adult party fun item. She (surely it'a a she) would be derned handy, maybe, at writing columns for us. Naturally we would have to curb that spicy tendency a little bit but where she got too spicy we could delete that part and insert a jug of buttermilk and three or four bullfrogs.

YES, ON SECOND THOUGHT we are very glad to have a Fun of the Month Club started. And it gives us another idea or two. For instance, a Sadness of the Month Club. If you have nothing to be sad about this club will come around and clout you once a month. Or this might be worked in with a Disease of the Month Club. When you join it each month you are sent a fresh supply of lovely disease germs, all different, all hearty,' all virulent but nonfatal. With a bonus, at the end of the year, of your choice of lockjaw or leprosy.

The original advertisement in a 1949 issue of *1000 Jokes Magazine*.

Shane's dice always rolled a 7 or 11!

The beginnings of Rochester's most notorious prankster

Myron Scheingold was born to Polish immigrants in Cincinnati on January 21, 1873. Twenty-eight years later, he married Sarah Goldstone and not long afterwards, their eldest son, Leroy Scheingold was born. Leroy's younger siblings would arrive later: Clara, Raymond and Evelyn.

By all accounts, Myron was a community-minded local small-businessman. At just twenty-one he ran for a position on the Cincinnati city council and as chairman of the Main Street Merchants' and Clerks' Association, he personally responded to letters from those in need. In 1914 he orchestrated the Christmas poor box and co-ordinated the distribution of 3,600 baskets to the city's neediest. He also agitated for the creation of a fund to support area unemployed towards a goal of $18,000.

Leroy Shane, *circa* 1976 (Photo via ancestry.com)

For years he was the proprietor of both the Star Cloak and Suit Company and Clara's Children's Shop across the street which Leroy managed in 1922. Unfortunately, a year later both were in bankruptcy proceedings and auction. Evidently the family tried to save the business but in 1925, Leroy's mother, who then owned Clara's, was liquidating and in bankruptcy proceedings. Afterwards, Myron became a furniture salesman. He died on November 9, 1930.

One of Leroy's earliest jobs, at 18, was as a candy store salesman; but even then he demonstrated business acumen as a partner in the Scheingold and (Otto J) Oechslin bakery.

As late as 1930, Leroy was still living at home but by 1937, he had moved to Little Rock, Arkansas and changed his name from Scheingold to Shane.

In Little Rock, Shane worked as a salesman for Pioneer Wholesale Liquor perhaps an incubator for his interest in barware. Shane married Elizabeth Sheppard on March 13, 1937 though very little else is known of this marriage or Shane's time in Little Rock. In 1937 and 1938 he was listed in city directories with Clara, perhaps she was his sister Clara.

In 1941, just prior to Shane's serendipitous visit to Rochester, Shane was living in Topeka, Kansas working for the Pueblo, Colorado National Broom Manufacturing Company.

Leroy Shane's 1978 death notice reported that he moved to Phoenix 15 years prior and may have maintained dual residencies to be near his mother Sarah who lived there until she died in 1972.

Shane began divesting himself of his catalog business in Rochester as early as the late 50's

Leroy Shane took advantage of some downtime on his sales job at the National Broom Manufacturing Company to check-in for a check-up at the Mayo Clinic.

and immediately after the first great Rochester flood in 1974, he permanently left the Med City.

He married his former partner Mabel Evenson (b. November 17, 1908) on May 7, 1972 in Imperial County California. She died in July of 1975 in Phoenix.

On June 18, 1976, Leroy married Ruth D. Kucera in Las Vegas, Nevada.

Leroy Shane died in Phoenix on January 19, 1978.

Who owns the moniker The Shepherd of the Sand Hills?

Shane fancied the sobriquet *The Shepherd of the Sand Hills* (sometimes "*Sandhills*") and used it not just to refer to himself, but as the name of his souvenir shop and as the by-name from whence many products in his enterprise originated.

But where, one might ask, did that "sonorous title," as the Rochester Post-Bulletin's Bill Holmes called it pondering in (or about) a 1957 profile, originate?

"The gadget monarch steadfastly refuses to disclose the origin," Holmes wrote, "and the ordinarily loquacious Mr. Shane abruptly clams up when questioned."

Ray Raver, who joined Shane as a salesman in 1957 and drove with him visiting potential retail outlets in the upper Midwest believes the name derived from the frequent sand storms Shane would encounter that took the paint off his truck.

One man who cared less about the name's genesis than its similarity to his own was a Rochester, New York, fellow named Charles Shepard who in 1943 filed an opposition to Shane's attempt to trademark *The Shepherd of the Sand Hills*.

In his objection, Shepard claimed Shane's registration would cause confusion in trade with his own product, a printed genealogical chart.

Shane's notation of *The Shephard of the Sand Hills* would be applied to, his original filing said, "necklaces made of nuts, wood, corn, animal horn, bone, leather and combinations thereof; ornamental pins made of nuts, fruit and coniferous substances."

Evidently, the *Examiner of Interferences* was unpersuaded by Shepard's objection and dismissed it in 1947.

Long before there were healthy choices and lean cuisines there were "Diets of Rochester"

Though the beginning of the modern frozen food era is generally marked by Clarence Birdseye's invention of "flash freezing" in 1927, it wasn't until 1944 that William Maxson created the frozen dinner — first for the military and then for commercial airlines.

More than a quarter of a century after Birdseye's process, domestic applications were still impractical because while as many as 70% of American homes had a refrigerator, few had a freezer. That changed rapidly and by 1954, the year Swanson introduced the iconic *TV Dinner*, more than twenty-five million frozen dinners were sold.

About that same time, another craze was sweeping the nation: dieting. That's when Leroy Shane saw an opportunity in the convergence of the two. The *Minneapolis Star* newspaper reported that "a man with a weight problem has converted his difficulty into a growing business. After a trip through Mayo Clinic," they wrote, "he was referred to the *Diet Kitchen* for a diet of 1,000 calories a day. Leroy Shane came up with the idea of packaging low-calorie frozen foods."

Colette Heise

In 1956, Leroy Shane forged a $10,000 test market program with Marshall Field's in Chicago and *Diets of Rochester*, the very first frozen diet dinner company in the nation, was born.

The original plan, as told to the *Star Tribune* in 1956, called for 1,000 calorie double packs offering a choice of 40 menus or combinations. Paul Pappas, the famed chef at Mantorville, Minnesota., whose Hubbell House is still in operation, was to do the cooking. The packaging would be done in nearby Kasson, Minn.

By the time the meals were rolled-out in October of 1957, things had changed significantly. Eight 275-calorie *Dream Diets* were created by Colette Heise who was a dietician at Methodist Hospital (Heise was also associated, for a time, with the *Rochester Diet Kitchen*, located in the Curie Hospital at 111 1st Street SW).

Each dinner consisted of hot and cold portions in revolutionary packaging (one side heated, the other defrosted) and included a vegetable, salad, dessert, and one of either broiled chicken, pork tenderloin, Swiss steak, breaded veal, roast beef, breaded haddock, macaroni scallopine, or diced beef in gravy. The dinners were manufactured by Tony Downs Foods in St. James, near Mankato, Minnesota, and Fist Brokerage Co., of Minneapolis, handled distribution.

Service was expanded a month later to include the Twin Cities. Operations between the two markets were combined and the company was headed by Sam S. Badali, one of the Midwest's pioneer frozen food processors. Shane was vice president and Heise the head dietician. The launch included several full-page full-color ads in Twin Cities' newspapers.

Advertising magazine *Tide* reported that Shame's promotional budget for the launch of the "competitively-priced" 79¢ dinners was $500,000, about $4.7 million in today's dollars!

Preparation of the *Dream Diet* meals was simple, in fact, that was their attraction. Warming simply required the entrée and vegetable pouch boil in water for 15 minutes to cook. Included with each *Dream Diet* were suggestions for various sensible breakfasts. Adhering to a 1,000-calorie diet simply required two of the frozen meals and one of the breakfasts described on the product package.

Shane created a jingle and the meals were heavily promoted by legendary pitchman Aaron Cushman who had before then represented institutions like *Century 21*, *Keebler Cookies*, and for a time, The Three Stooges. Newspapers from Reading, Pennsylvania to Oxnard, California and from Mason City, Iowa to St. Petersburg, Florida cited the introduction of these culinary wonders.

Locally, the lunchroom of Shane's novelty manufacturing facility on North Broadway was transformed into an *ad hoc* test kitchen. Erika Austin worked for Shane in those days and recalled that the lounge was always stocked with the dinners. "They tasted good," she said, "for diet food."

The following year, Diets of Rochester appointed Bruce C. Hartman executive sales manager. Hartman came from dinner giant Holloway House Frozen Food and prepared to expand distribution to the Milwaukee area but there is no evidence that actually happened.

Unfortunately, *Diets of Rochester* never gained traction and faded-away. That there were some allegations the dinners traded on the Mayo Clinic

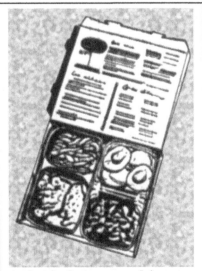

A sketch that appeared in some newspapers of the time promoting the Dream Diet. Clockwise from the bottom left: meat entrée, vegetable, dessert, and salad. One side heated, the other side defrosted.

name or that of the similarly titled "Rochester Diet Kitchen" played no part. Shane was simply ahead of his time. It would be nearly 30 years — in 1985 with the introduction of ConAgra's "Healthy Choice" — before the industry fully-embraced the diet frozen dinners he pioneered.

Today, nutrition-themed frozen dinners are ubiquitous — we chill-out with more than one and a half billion of them each year. But there was a time when they were a novelty. And an innovation. And it all started in Rochester, Minnesota.

A promotional photo for Diets of Rochester's *Dream Diet* frozen dinners. © Diets of Rochester.

A promotional photo for Diets of Rochester's *Dream Diet* frozen dinners. © Diets of Rochester.

COLOR

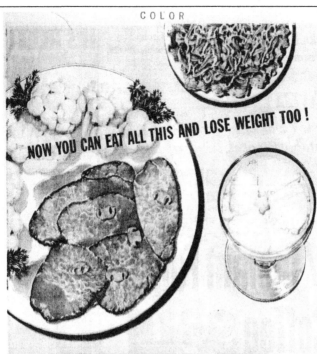

NOW YOU CAN EAT ALL THIS AND LOSE WEIGHT TOO!

IF YOU LOVE TO EAT... BUT MUST LOSE WEIGHT...

dream diet

FULL-COURSE FROZEN DINNERS

IMAGINE! ONLY 275 CALORIES IN EACH DELICIOUS MEAL!

Now you can enjoy hearty, full-course meals... even dessert... and still lose up to 2 pounds a week! New Dream Diet frozen dinners make reducing as easy as sitting down to a delicious meal... actually fill you up without filling you out. Best of all, Dream Diets are so downright delicious you'd buy them for flavor alone. The Diets of Rochester has taken favorite gourmet recipes of outstanding chefs and created taste-tempting dinners that contain only 275 calories... yet provide you with all the balanced nourishment you need for healthy, active living. You actually eat your way slim... because the *calories are controlled*. If you don't agree that this is the most sensible way to reduce... just ask your doctor!

CHOICE OF 8 TASTE-TEMPTING MEALS

FROM THE HEALTH CENTER OF THE WORLD TO YOUR GROCER'S FROZEN FOOD SECTION

ROCHESTER DIETITIANS RELEASE FIRST FROZEN DIET DINNERS

Only 275 Calories In New Dream Diet Full-Course Meals

AUTHORITIES AGREE ON MOST SENSIBLE WAY TO LOSE WEIGHT

NEW FROZEN DINNERS CREATED BY DIETS OF ROCHESTER

**November 15, 1957 full-page full-color introductory advertisement.
© 1957 Diets of Rochester.**

The Slinky® first walked down stairs in Rochester, Minnesota

Or it didn't.
It all depends on which lore one finds more plausible.

The official origin of the iconic spring toy goes something like this:
A young engineer named Richard James, a recent Penn State graduate, was working for the venerable Cramp's Shipyard. Though they had been in operation since 1830, Cramp's had never been busier. It was 1943 and in the midst of World War II, our government was demanding cruisers and battleships as fast as the Philadelphia shipyard could produce them.

James was a "guarantee engineer," essentially validating that specifications were adhered to and performance met commitments – specifically with regards to marine torsion meters. These meters required a steady platform[1] on which to operate with springs dampening the various vibrations (rough seas, gunfire recoil, etc...) that might otherwise impact their performance.

---

[1] By some accounts, the meters were "suspended" by springs, by others, the devices rested on them.

Consequently, James found himself a frequent passenger on the test cruises of these Navy war ships experimenting with springs and spring configurations to improve methods of stabilizing these sensitive instruments.

Because different spring designs offered different advantages – for instance, a spring wound from flat wire would

"I'll Look for You to Be Here Saturday"

Santa Claus likes nothing better than to have boys and girls tell him what they want for Christmas. He'd like to have his picture taken with the little folks; Mother will like them as keepsake gifts, and they cost only 49c.

TOYLAND—BALCONY

Little Folks Love These Cuddly Toys

Soft, cuddly stuffed animals that every young child loves and doesn't want to let go of, and here in a big variety—Teddy bears, dogs, bambi, pandas—$2.25 to $4.95.

Here's Slinky!

Slinky always wants to go down . . . a toy that will fascinate and amuse the whole family. Spring steel—priced at $1.00.

TOYLAND—BALCONY

Wakauwa, the Animated Dog Also Barks!

He wags his tail, turns his head, lies down, and barks!— this most amusing of all toys. He's made of polished wood; all joints are movable. Press the bottom of the block and he performs. A toy that can be manipulated by children, and that keeps oldsters amused. $1.00.

TOYLAND—BALCONY

A portion of a Christmas season advertisement for "The Palace" department store in Spokane, Washington. This December 1946 illustration is one of the earliest known and represents the countrywide appeal of the Slinky.

stand more reliably than one wound from round wire – James' desk was typically cluttered with many different designs.

As luck would have it, on one fateful day, one of the springs fell off James' desk performing some odd contortions along the way.

With a young son at home, James saw potential for a toy. For two years he toiled with various designs and in the summer of 1945, he was ready to unveil what his wife Betty coined the "Slinky."

The James' invested in a small run of the toys and quickly sold out, first in a local toyshop, then again, with a larger inventory at an area department store. Nothing before was so fascinating. This simple spring could walk down an incline or a set of stairs!

Almost overnight it became a craze, and just as quickly, other manufactures followed with their own spring toys. All of them manufactured by different companies and in different cities.

James filed for a patent in August of 1946[2], but because so many knock-offs mushroomed so quickly he doubted one would be granted. But in January of 1947, James was granted patent # 2,415,012.

James Industries continued to thrive under Richard's leadership until 1960 when he abruptly walked away from his family and the company he founded in order to follow a religious cult[3] to Bolivia, leaving Betty to run the company.

James Industries, Inc., the company Richard and Betty James founded, was eventually sold – its place in toy infamy intact. At its peak they sold millions of Slinkys and by 1948 had licensed the design to three manufacturers, two in the United States and one in Canada. The first to license the Slinky was Leroy Shane.[4]

---

[2] The patent process likely began earlier. James noted in his patent application that it was a "continuation" of his November 1945 application for a "toy and process."

[3] Another equally unsubstantiated version of Richard James' exodus is that he followed the Christian organization "Wycliffe Bible Translators."

[4] As recalled by Betty James in an interview with writer Robert Braham, author of the definitive history and technology of the Slinky titled, "The Single Helix."

Piston Ring Toys

"The walking coil business is booming...with a
half dozen manufacturers advertising nationally."
—Tide magazine, *1947*

By the time James' patent was granted in 1947 the market was saturated with what were then collectively referred to as "piston ring toys." Said Tide magazine, a trade publication for advertising and marketing executives, "The talented piston ring that walks downstairs, coils and hisses like a snake, makes like a yo-yo and otherwise astonishes and delights all ages has been selling well for the past two years."

Piston rings toys?

As early as early as 1945, James noted the Slinky resembled a stack of piston rings, which are used in engines to seal a piston to the cylinder wall within which it operates.

Historically, many materials and several methods have been employed to create these rings which were typically cast from iron or machined on a lathe.

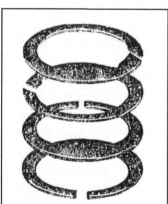

A stack of piston rings. Illustration from Haling's patent application.

Another technique, a newer one, involved simply cutting the rings from a coil of preformed flat steel wire, a coil that looks strikingly similar to the Slinky.

Some might say, then – indeed some have, as we'll soon see – that credit for the invention of the toy ought rightfully belong to the inventor of the machine that manufactured piston ring coils.

But as Yale Professor W. J. Cunningham noted in a 1947 article in *The American Journal of Physics* titled, "The Physics of the Tumbling Spring," there is a lot more to this novelty than meets the eye (of piston ring operators).

Still, the similarity to the coils kicked-out of machine shops across the country did not go unnoticed.[5]

As quickly as James' device became available, other manufacturers, many of them spring or piston ring makers, introduced toys of their own.

By all accounts, longtime Philadelphia piston ring maker Wilkening Manufacturing Company was the most successful of the Slinky competitors. Their "Mr. Wiggle" and its offspring[6] (*teehee*) were popular through the late 1950s.

"Mr. Wiggle" was one of the more successful piston ring toys. Made by Wilkening Manufacturing Company, whose line was popular well into the 1950s, it was essentially a Slinky-like spring. Images on its box could be cutout and inserted between coils to make a face and feet.

Other walking toys included Association Spring Corporation's "Wiggly Wag dog," whose trademark was unsuccessfully opposed by Wilkening.

Smalley Accessories Corporation's Travis Products Company, maker of piston rings and small engines, manufactured a "Mr. Walker," though there is little evidence it was available for any significant length of time.

---

[5] Depending on the credibility of the various Slinky hagiographies, the lines of innovation either converge at or disperse from a piston ring machine. One thing is definite, steel piston rings lasted longer and manufacturers of those rings needed alternate products to sustain their production facilities.

[6] Wilkening's line also included "Mr. Wiggle's Turtle," "Leap Frog," "Cata-Puller," "Cowboy," "Alligator," and "Bunny," all likely as a response to James Industries' "Slinky Dog" introduced in 1952. Slinky introduced other "dogs," as well, i.e., less-successful variations like the Slinky Flying Saucer and the Slinky Satellite Beanie.

A 1946 advertisement for Shane's souvenir shop promoting his Magi-Koil as "The funniest, craziest, most fascinating 'Do-Dad' you've ever seen."

Barely on the radar were the "Walkie-coil" and the "Quirly."

Noteworthy of the piston ring toys, was the one promoted and wholesaled by Leroy Shane of Rochester, Minnesota. The one he called the "Magi-Koil[7]."

The Magi-Koil

When word of Richard James' invention reached a small machine shop on SE 3rd avenue in Rochester, Minnesota, 1100 miles from Philadelphia, Otto Haling was unimpressed. Haling had been sweeping away coils like James' Slinky for years.

In 1934 Haling invented the machine to make a flat coil from round wire from which to clip new rings piston rings. These flat coils were the progenitors of spring toys though he was oblivious to their entertainment value.

Shane knew Haling — their shops were just blocks apart — in fact, the inventor manufactured the Magi-Koils for him.

This is where it becomes apparent that the history of the Slinky®, indeed all spring toys, is far from settled.

It's reasonable to conclude that if the toy was the byproduct of a machine, the inventor of that machine ought to get some credit?

Maybe.

---

[7] Sometimes "Magic Coil," or "Magi-Coil."

But a lot of people observed the same thing once James' toy took-off. In fact, many piston ring manufactures observed the same thing: that the flat coils fell, wavered, maybe even danced between their hand or their children's.

Still, if Haling invented the machine that most manufacturers used to create those coils, he was likely the first to watch them walk, or at least stumble, away from one of them. James, however, managed to get them to walk all the way to toy department shelves by creating a buzz and securing a patent.

What exactly is a Leaping Lena?

Shane called his

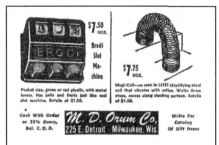

Above: A 1946 ad for the *Magi-Koil* which Leroy Shane both retailed and wholesaled.

Below: An advertisement from Shane's wholesale catalog ca. 1950. What was originally the *Magi-Koil* was now, under license from James Industries, the *Slinky Magic Coil*.

780—SLINKY MAGIC COIL
Sensational Toy that does everything. Walks down steps, coils and recoils like a snake. Dressed up in the new 1950 colors, red, green, yellow, blue. Neatly boxed. Backed by enormous amount of national publicity and advertising.
$7.20 Doz
6 Doz quantities, $6.90 Doz

Magi-Koil, a "Leaping Lena of Swedish Steel" but the etymology of the alliterative pop culture reference of the time is not obvious.

For example, *Leaping Lena* was a popular champion jumping horse on the steeplechase circuit in the 1930's and the name of a California state-fair frog-jumping winner.

A giant pickerel was called by anglers a *Leaping Lena* as was the controversial sister/manager of professional boxer "Kingfish" Levinsky.

One town changed the name of a women's callisthenic to *Leaping Lena* from the prosaic Jumping Jack while another's all-male basketball team were, oddly, the *Leaping Lenas*.

Perhaps it was merely common parlance or a homage to the Norwegians of the area and their *Ole and Lena jokes* that inspired the moniker.

Only the Shepherd of the Sand Hills knows.

Left: A 1925 newspaper reported the advent of a dangerous new cocktail that was said to "imbibe drinkers with a desire to precipitate themselves from diving boards, balconies, cliffs or other high places." Right: A 1926 advertisement for the *Leaping Lena* candy bar.

Swedish Steel: What's the deal?

In the nascent days of spring toys, the mark of quality for any manufactured product was evidently "Swedish steel." Ostensibly, for the past half-century, it was heralded as the best steel in the world.

The quality of Swedish steel, the boast went, is rooted in the "purity of Swedish ore." Swedish steel was smoother and more pliant; it was "soft but tough."

Because its "elastic life after being tempered seemed unlimited" it was perfectly suited for razor blades, watch springs and coil springs. It could twist 20 times without breaking.

Whether or not Swedish steel was actually better than U.S. Steel is irrelevant. It was perceived as the cat's pajamas of metals and Shane, quick to capitalize on the craze *du jour*, shrewdly highlighted it as the material from which his Magi-Koil was made.

From top left: 1922 razor, 1950 rifle, Shane's Magi-Koil, 1933 garden hoe, 1933 roller skates, 1946 knives, 1925 umbrella ribs.

A million dollars out the window

By Roy J. Dunlap. From the Feb. 15, 1948 St. Paul Sunday Pioneer Press. Reprinted with permission

Otto Haling, Rochester inventor, holds one of the steel coils which cost him a million dollars when he "failed to recognize the darn thing had value as a toy."

Otto Haling still can smile after tossing a million dollars out the window. The Rochester, Minnesota, inventor, machine designer and piston ring manufacturer, unknowingly fashioned a toy in 1934 which caught the nation's fancy 12 years later and netted another man a fortune.

It all began when Otto, seeking to speed production in his backyard factory, invented and patented a machine to produce coils from strip steel. Otto cut the coils to form laminated rings for automotive engines.

In 1946 an eastern engineer, studying one of the machines Otto had sold to another company, took a coil home to amuse his children. One of the youngsters accidentally dropped it at the top of a stairway. The coil compressed, expanded and actually walked downstairs!

Toy manufacturers snapped at the novelty and the engineer settled back while the money rolled in from the breadth of America.

Otto read about the find in a national magazine and rummaged under a workbench where he had thrown several imperfect coils years before. "I just sat there looking at a million dollars in my hands," he grins. "That's what a man gets for wrapping himself up in inventing and forgetting the merchandising angle."

Otto's passion for inventing has cost him money in other ways, he confesses, "but that's the way I am, spending more time inventing than I do making money."

Right now he's working on a jet turbine engine which "will develop 150 horsepower, weigh 100 pounds and take up as much room as a suitcase. If it works as I expect it to, I'll forget about that other million dollars I lost in the coil toy."

The 47-year-old inventor was born on a farm near Rochester where he drove his father to distraction "tinkering around with machinery more than farming." Completing high school in Rochester he moved to Waterloo, Iowa, to work for a tractor company. While there he invented and patented a tractor carburetor which reduced weight of the unit from nine and one-half to three and one-half pounds and provided less fuel consumption in the bargain. According to Otto the company still uses his carburetor on its latest models.

Tiring of working for someone else, Otto returned to Rochester in 1925 and opened a machine shop in part of a chicken hatchery. He worked on carburetor problems for eight years, financing himself by doing garage work and designing technical machine for manufacturers.

"I gave up carburetors in 1933," he says, "convinced that the peak of fuel efficiency had been reached with present engines."

He began the manufacture of piston rings next, designing laminated rings and inventing another ring which cuts down oil consumption in an old engine.

The Magi-Koil. (From the author's collection.)

The TravLers' Trading Post

Cruise to a *Speedway*, *Kwik Trip* or most any other popular chain and what you might not have noticed is that gasoline is often the least-advertised product sold there. Stations today carry so much more than thin-sales-margined petroleum products. Found now are items like bananas, iPhone cases, compression socks, and even their own store-label jerky. Need something in a pinch? Chances are you can get it close by at one of these ubiquitous convenience marts.

But it wasn't always like that. In gas stations of yore, and even those of not so yore, you got one thing: gas.

If you needed a fresh razor or tube of toothpaste, that was a trip in town to a drug store or supermarket.

Leroy Shane spent a lot of time travelling the state highways in the upper Midwest stocking souvenir shops from Mt. Rushmore to the Wisconsin Dells and one thing he found lacking was quick access to the necessities of life.

His solution: the *TravLers' Trading Post*, an 8-foot by 3-foot portable shop for gas stations, motels, or other remote outposts where space was at a minimum.

The *TravLers' Trading Post* stocked 50 items chosen by a local druggist deemed most essential and Shane and his general manager Phil Sternberg selected 200 souvenirs and gifts which could also be stocked.

Shane commissioned Crenlo VP and assistant chief engineer Stuart Haessly to fabricate it.

"We wanted it made of steel so vandals couldn't damage it too much," Shane explained to the Pioneer Press News Service. It took only a minute to close the unit and another minute to open it for business. Closed, it could be padlocked.

Evidently, the *TravLers' Trading Post* made its debut at the Minnesota State Fair but nothing seemed to come of it.

Newspaper reprint of Leroy Shane and his *TravLers' Trading Post* with opened panels extending their display. Photo © Rochester Post-Bulletin. Used with permission.

Barware

The so-called *man cave* is neither a new nor a novel concept. Though today's variant might include high-end electronics or expensive vintage vending- or gambling-machines, the purpose and vibe is no different from those basements or garage-corners of the 1950's, 60's or 70's which boasted a homemade bar and a few local light-up beer signs. They were and are a place to relax and hold court after a long day at the office or mill.

Shane keenly understood this market and what was not souvenir-related in his catalogs were generally accouterments for these home sanctuaries — those private domains where one could carry on both earthy and unapologetically. Accessories for them were appreciated by the men (it was always men) who valued and shared that which could induce a hearty laugh. In fact, Shane himself would admit that when it came to these gags, he was customer #1.

Even then, or especially then, many of these items had a whiff of naughtiness hiding behind a double entendre. Some were single entendres. A few were arguably racially insensitive while others required no argument at all, they *were* racially insensitive. In mixed company, one would look over both shoulders before mentioning or presenting them, but in one's own home tavern, they were prominently displayed.

Collectively they were known as barware, though the term generally includes practical utensils as well like corkscrews and muddlers.

Shane's most popular item in this category was the "Bar Boy Bib."

The Bar Boy Bib

Perhaps the Bar Boy Bib best illustrated Shane's irreverent hodgepodge approach to humor: if it's funny, make it work.

The Bar Boy Bib was an apron replete with gags in its many pockets. Several of those included overlapped with Fun of the Month Club items including the bib itself.

For a time, a Bar Boy Bib hung in The Museum of the American Cocktail in New Orleans.

In its peak period, 1949-1952, advertisements for the Bar Boy Bib appeared in publications across the country, especially around Father's Day and Christmas.

The aprons themselves were all over the place. Literally. Actually. Erika Austin, who worked in Shane's plant for years, remembered they were frequently used as smocks to keep their clothes clean.

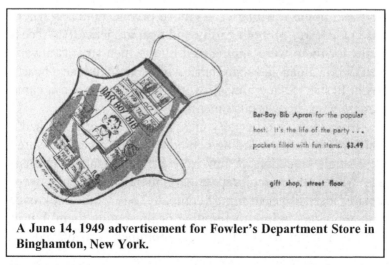

Bar-Boy Bib Apron for the popular host. It's the life of the party . . . pockets filled with fun items. **$3.49**

gift shop, street floor

A June 14, 1949 advertisement for Fowler's Department Store in Binghamton, New York.

In my own collection, I have five of them including a military-themed one and a month does not go by that another doesn't pop-up on eBay.

The basic bib

There are some minor variations, but the average bib contained pockets for House Dice (constructed to always throw

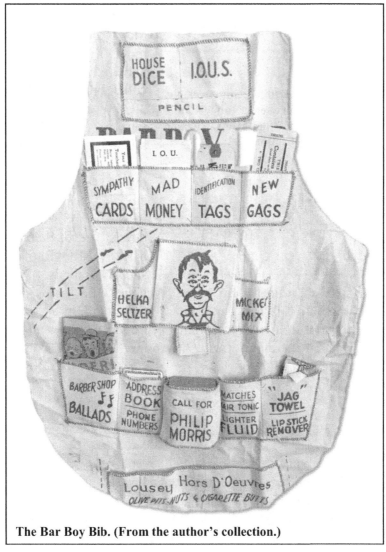

The Bar Boy Bib. (From the author's collection.)

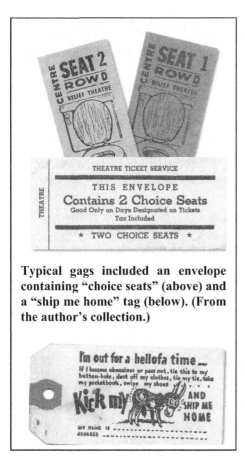

Typical gags included an envelope containing "choice seats" (above) and a "ship me home" tag (below). (From the author's collection.)

7's or 11's); gag I.O.U.s; a pencil; sympathy cards ("Your story has touched my heart, Never before have I met anyone with more troubles than you, Please accept this token of my sincerest sympathy"); Mad money (play money); an "ID" card to be fixed to a drunk's collar button reading: "If I become obnoxious or pass out, tie this to my button-hole, dust off my clothes, tie my tie, take my pocketbook, swipe my shoes ... and ship me home;" *Helka* Seltzer; Mickey Mix; Barbershop Ballads; an address book; a tin for cigarettes; "Matches, Hair Tonic and Lighter Fluid" (what could go wrong there?); a "Jag" towel/lipstick remove (essentially a printed napkin); and a large pouch for "Lousey *Hors D'Oeuvres* – Olive pits, nuts & cigarette butts."

The G.I. Utility Bib-M1 edition

The military variant packaged several of the same gags but under a military theme. It sported a few sayings like "Grab your sox, men, it's 0530!" and contained pockets for: Identification K-9 Dog Tags; gag cards for chow, ration, hot poker, I.O.U. and T/S (an acronym that translates roughly to "too bad for you"); Kits; Field Pack; Section 8 material; Good Ole Sarge – The Old S.O.B. – Son of Battle; Gold Brick Supplies; Witty Ditties for Servicemen and officers; Date bait of last resort (cash); Bouncing Bettys and Maggie's Drawers (the former a nick-name for landmines and the latter an expression for someone who was a poor rifleman); a large pouch labelled "Nomenclature d'snafu – Frugal - pronounced "fragile" - French: CS – Chicken Soup, SOS – Soup on a Shingle, OCS

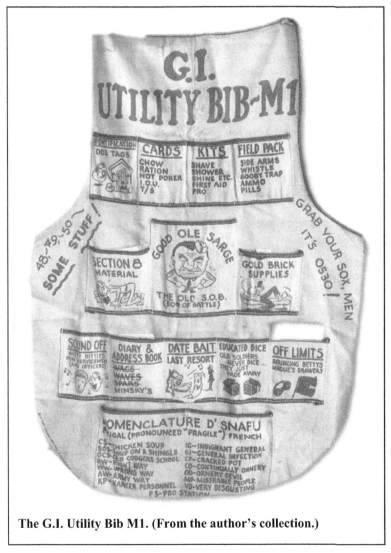

The G.I. Utility Bib M1. (From the author's collection.)

– Old Codgers School, RW – Right Way, WW – Wrong Way, AW – Army Way, KP – Kancer Personnel, IG – Indignant General, GI – General Infection, CP – Cracked pot, CO – Continually Ornery, OD – Ornery Devil, MP – Miserable People, VD – Very disgusting, PS – Pro Station.

The G.I. Utility Bib-M1 also included without explanation a clownish roll-out tie greater than the length of the entire bib.

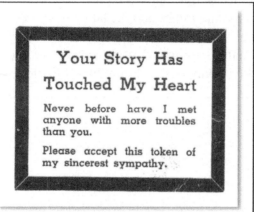

Your Story Has Touched My Heart

Never before have I met anyone with more troubles than you.

Please accept this token of my sincerest sympathy.

There was overlap between gags included in the *Fun of the Month Club* and both bibs. For instance, the text of the Bar Boy Bib's sympathy card (above) is repurposed for the *Official T/S card* (below). (From the author's collection.)

OFFICIAL T/S CARD, - MI

Your story has touched my heart. Never before have I met anyone with more troubles than you. Please accept this token of my sincerest sympathy.

You are now a recognized member of the Official T/S CLUB, AUS; USN, USMC, AAF, WAC, WAVES, SPARS.

I hereby set my name and punch.

Holy Joe, Chaplain

Capt., AUS

GRIPE CHART

Punch Here

☐ Latrine Duty	☐ Wife Trouble
☐ Aching Back	☐ Money Trouble
☐ Lousy Chow	☐ In-Law Trouble
☐ Crumby Deals	☐ Just Plain Trouble

Gag Naps

While the cocktail is a relatively recent concoction — developed largely to temper the harsh taste of poorly- and hurriedly-distilled spirits during the prohibition era — the cocktail napkin goes back quite a bit further.

Historians specializing in the Medieval period have discovered small cloths they believe were used for that purpose packed among what appears to be poker supplies in a locked box under Arthur's round table. (Also found were *markers* signed by Sagramore and Perceval, evidently unpaid, and a notepad with sketches titled "Merlin's card tricks – Do not read under penalty of combustion.")

On several of the cloths were etchings of Guinevere, Morgawse, and the Lady of the Lake with comically-enlarged bosoms and captions like, "From wench it came," and, "Mulberry gin? Bring more in!" One depicts a knight weeping at the rear of a bent-over large-posteriored maiden wiping spilled mead from the castle floor lamenting, "Methinks the lady doth protest not nearly enough."

OK, so maybe we don't actually know for sure what those more than a thousand years ago found funny but we can guess there are certain themes that are timeless to those lifting a mug of ale; Leroy Shane tapped into that in the early 1950s with his *Gag Naps*.

Hilarious

GAG NAPS

Comic Cocktail Napkins

Your Guests Will Scream!

Reg. $1.00 Pkg. of 50 **48c**

Old Time Bargain Special!

"Your Guests Will Scream!" An advertisement in the August 4, 1952 Wausau Daily Herald for Fox Cut Rate Drugs (located next to Kresge's, in case you were curious). Note: 40¢ in 1952 is approximately $4.75 in today's dollars.

Gag Naps were comic cocktail napkins packed 50 to a box (later 15 in a cellophane sleeve).

Then, as now, the market was crowded with such gags and no portable home bar was without them. Shane's were developed in 1951 and heavily marketed in 1952 across the country. By 1953 they were discounted and packaged in smaller packages.

That many of these cheeky napkins survived is a testament to either their popularity or to so many of them being so well secreted away.

Gag Naps. (From the author's collection.)

The Crying Towel, Smarty Pants and more

Amateur or professional, a barkeep is a magnet for tales of woe.

How then is a mixologist expected to keep a dry tabletop under so much sobbing?

Ironically, in 1930, the first year of the Great Depression, a solution emerged to soak-up those crocodile tears — then for businessmen but in later years for anyone in need of commiseration, from fishermen and athletes to henpecked husbands: the *Crying Towel*.

M.U. Cager Jim McCoy Can Stand on Own Rep

Tom Hearden, left, of the University of Wisconsin and Bill Fischer of Notre Dame exchanged condolences Saturday at the Good Fellers Dinner. Hearden points to the "We wus robbed" section of the "Krying Towel" as he and Fischer talk over the poor seasons at their respective universities. Both predicted better days in 1957. © 1956 Racine Journal Times.

The December 10, 1930 *Montana Standard* heralded the crying towel thusly:

The "crying towel" has made its appearance.

A local business house is having them distributed as "an aid to business." The towel is of absorbent paper and bears the inscription: "Crying Towel. Let's all lie down and howl about business, it will help so much."

There is the further suggestion that "the next bozo who comes weeping to you, crying 'bad business' just hand him

Leroy Shane's *Krying Towel* c. 1951.

this towel, direct him to a quiet corner, and tell him to 'go to it.'

"When the lachrymose fluid[8] has performed its functions, he may be able to see things in a better light. The 'crying towel' is said to be meeting with favor in Butte business circles."

Toilet humor and ladies' underwear being the stapes of the pre-adolescent sense of humor tucked deep into a lot of grown men, Shane introduced the Party Briefs apron in 1952 as the "Smarty Pants" apron.

An advertisement from the March 3, 1952 issue of *Billboard* magazine for Shane's *Smarty Pants*.

---

[8] I looked it up so you don't have to: Tears.

The February 23, 1952 *Billboard* heralded it as, "the hit of the Chicago Gift Show," but by December it was discounted, though still well-described in that publication:

Leroy Shane, Inc., is offering the "Smarty Pants" cocktail apron, cut in the shape of panties, at a new low price of $9.60 a dozen. It is made of black material with screened white lettering and white lace decorations. Inscribed on it in white lettering are such gags as "dangerous curves ahead" and "tie me to your apron strings again."

Party Briefs, a likely later variant of the *Smarty Pants*. (From the author's collection.)

Shane's wholesale catalogs included several bar-related items. Many were standards like "the strip tease glass" ("clothes come off when glass is filled") and, for the art lover, Jérôme Duquesnoy the Elder's *Brussels Boy* atop an ashtray who "actually puts out your cigarette. No more burnt furniture."

Others included:

The "Outhouse cigarette dispenser" — "Pull the chain and cigarette pops out. *Practical* novelty for den, recreation room or bar."

Crooked martini glass — "Souvenir of my bender."

Witty gag plaques — "Please remain seated while the room is in motion!"

Clockwise from top. A witty gag plaque; Brussels Boy cigarette extinguisher; crooked bender glass; "practical" cigarette dispenser.

Coonskin caps 'n powder horns

It was a popular thing in my youth to dress for Halloween as Davy Crockett. It wasn't that we were fans as much as it gave us an excuse to walk around the neighborhood with our BB guns.[9]

However, a decade before we were trick-or-treating to any house giving full-size *3 Musketeers* bars for as many times as until we were recognized as *repeaters*, coonskin caps were ubiquitous. In fact, it is impossible to overstate their popularity in the 1950s.

Some say this was because of Disney's successful *Davy Crockett* TV series, others say it wasn't Fess Parker's version of "The King of the Wild Frontier"

Though it was only a political campaign stunt, this giant coonskin cap atop the Tennessee State Capitol in Nashville in 1952 was a testament to Crockett's legacy. Photo © 1952 *Nashville Banner.*

---

[9] I describe this and other escapades in my semi-autobiographical book *"Bless me, Father, for I have sinned..."* - *Anecdotes and Allocutions from Mr. Action.*

An actual coonskin cap made from an entire raccoon skin (above) looked quite a bit different from the sanitized children's version that was essentially a pillbox-style cap with a tail (below).

that stirred excitement but rather the series' chart-topping song, "The Ballad of Davy Crockett."

To Leroy Shane, it did not matter how the frenzy originated. It was just another "Sputnik is a no-goodnik;" another craze *du jour* on which to capitalize. His business acumen being what it was, he pivoted and as kids say, he totally *owned* it! As a June 1955 Rochester Post Bulletin profile reported:

[Shane had already sold tons of hats when] the Shane-Sternberg duo decided to convert a display room at the New Yorker hotel, New York City, into [a Native American] museum setting for the annual Toy Fair. In making up decorative items for the museum, they decided to use some horns from Texas longhorn cattle to call attention to one of their products, the Chief Black Hawk powder horn. Dick Sternberg, 12-year-old son of Phil, had become adept at polishing and trimming the cattle horns. In dressing up one of the large ones for display, he attached a raccoon tail. Visitors to the Shane display started referring to the creation as a Davy Crockett powder horn. They inquired about availability of the regular size horns as a Davy Crockett item. Shane and Sternberg quickly converted display kits on hand into Davy Crockett powder horn kits. Meanwhile they dreamed up a Davy Crockett vest with screened images and 'coon-tail trim. Orders for both items started mounting. Sternberg rushed back to Rochester before the fair ended to get production set-up.

> "The coonskin cap is the badge of pioneer extraction. The time was when the coonskin cap was to a rifle match and turkey raffle what a collapsible silk tile [*formal hat*] is to the foyer of Delmonico's restaurant."
>
> — *Lafayette Courier*
> December 31, 1914

The Crockett items have been sent to every state, to Canada, Mexico, and Hawaii. Since the opportunity was seized [earlier in the year] orders have snowballed to more than $300,000 [$2.9 million in today's dollars]. The country has been virtually scoured for adequate supplies of raccoon tails and cattle horns. At one time there were 45,000 tails on hand in Rochester. After consuming more than 50,000 cattle horns from every major and minor livestock market, the firm has been forced to switch to plastic horns.

The United State Commerce Department gets involved.

Officials at the Commerce Department are now scouring Latin America for lightweight cow horns. It seems there's a shortage of them in this country due to the terrific demand by juvenile Davy Crocketts for powder horns.

Leroy Shane, Inc. of Rochester, Minn., wrote in to the department asking for help on this problem. The firm said it has sold thousands and thousands of these accessories and had exhausted the supply of junior-size cow horns. Western horns are considered to be too heavy for kids.

— *Ironwood* [Michigan] *Daily Globe*
May 28, 1955

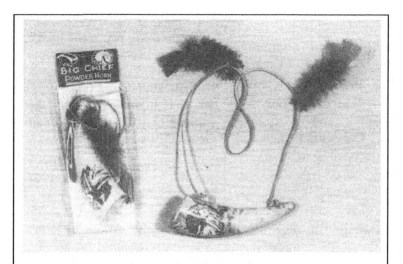

No. 1075 BIG CHIEF POWDER HORN

Plastic powder horn with sound, bright Indianhead decal, feathers, 2 color rayon neck cord. Good child's toy or souvenir.

No. 1075 Poly Package.....................$7.20 Doz.
No. 1075B Bulk Pack.........................$6.00 Doz.

After the Crockett craze played-out, the horns, now plastic, reverted to the *Big Chief Powder Horn* name. From Shane's 1957 wholesale catalog.

Tom-Tom Drums and ABC

In 1946, Leroy Shane desperately needed to *drum-up* some business.

Manufacturing supplies for toys were practically nonexistent during the Second World War while demand from national distributors for product, any toy product, was at an all-time high.

Shane and then VP and general manager Phil Sternberg were scratching their heads when serendipity pulled up to their SE Second Street shop.

"A battered old car loaded with children and tom-toms pulled up to the store." Sternberg related to the *Rochester Post-Bulletin* in 1957. "A Dakota from Prairie Island near Red Wing told Shane he and his family were making tom-toms."

The Dakota family had salvaged large tin cans from hotels and hospitals. Wood-grained wallpaper covered the cans and inner tubes were cut for drumheads. To complete the toys, they laced these rubber heads with twine and string.

The Native Americans' products intrigued Shane[10] and he he began selling them.

"It's quite a thrill," Sternberg admits, "to walk into a store in a city like New Orleans, Atlanta, Salt Lake City or

---

[10] Shane famously said, "We can take anything that's different."

Chicago and see these tom-toms on display. I've seen them in a store in the heart of Times Square in New York City and in little stores in out of the way places in northern Wisconsin and Upper Michigan."

A 1946 *Star Tribune* piece by George Grim was equally fascinated with Shane's new product line:

The tom-toms are more Shane than Big Chief, but they have boomed their way into the darnedest international market.

Most of the space upstairs in his 2nd Street shop is full of those "genuine Indian made Tom-Toms" in various sizes.

The tom-tom consists of a round, tin body, made for Shane by American Can. The heads are of rubber — old inner tubes, maybe, for smaller ones, any sheet rubber Shane can find for the bigger booms. The lacing is plastic.

Shane supplies the Prairie Island Dakota with the feather and the bead that goes with each tom-tom. To make the American Can look like birchbark, he sends to Prairie Island some birchbark wallpaper, which is pasted on the tin.

Anyhow, the Dakota DO make the tom-tom by assembling Shane's parts, then painting a genuine Indian war bonnet on the rubber head.[11]

"The Dakota supply their own paint," Shane says proudly. "And I don't know where they get it. It's scarce."

You feel that, somehow, Shane feels he ought to supply the paint, too.

Orders for the tom-toms have come from South Africa, Netherlands, West Indies, from department stores in New York, Chicago, and San Francisco.

In fact, "Shane was swamped with orders," Sternberg recalls. "The Prairie Island Dakota couldn't supply enough tom-toms to meet the demand. We gradually began making them ourselves."

---

[11] The emphasis here was Grim's but would prove prescient some twenty years later when the authenticity of Shane's *Indian Traders* line of products was oppugned.

One of Leroy Shane's *Big Chief Tom-Toms*. (From the author's collection.)

The impact to the local Rochester economy of the Big Chief line of tom-toms and related products like dolls and decorative headdresses could not be overstated.

Shane created a new organization, *Indian Traders*, to handle the distribution and his new plant on North Broadway was buzzing. At peak, it had about 57 local residents working on the day shift and another 25 on the swing shift and was one of the post office's best customers: in just the past few years, the Post-Bulletin reported, the postage meter had run up more than $30,000 ($292,000 in today's dollars).

Printing was done in three area shops and a company policy directed that all available equipment and supplies be purchased locally.

But even then, Shane struggled to meet demand.

"If only we could find someone to manufacture, oh, maybe fifty-thousand units…" He might have mulled.

About the time Shane's plant was running at capacity, IBM's Ken Zubay came to Rochester to develop a lab there.

Zubay would later serve in the Minnesota state legislature and prove instrumental in several civic improvements including the Soldiers Field Veterans Memorial. But his noblest legacy was arguably the Ability Building Center.

| Sept. 2, 1958 | LE ROY SHANE | 2,850,156 |

DRUM PACKAGE
Filed Sept. 13, 1954

FIG. 1   FIG. 2   FIG. 3   FIG. 4   FIG. 7   FIG. 5

INVENTOR.
LE ROY SHANE
BY
Chas. C. Reif
ATTORNEY

FIG. 6

Shane's 1958 patent was for a drum kit that permitted "a youngster the pleasure and the training of assembling the items to form a drum." The parts were hermetically sealed and required a can-opener to access.

"Industrial management," the *Minneapolis Morning Tribune* quoted him as saying, "is motivated by the self-preservation factor not to accept an unknown quantity [vis-à-vis special needs workers] for fear he will not work out."

This was a barrier for the disabled in their quest for gainful employment. The answer, Zubay said, was a sheltered workshop like the Ability Building Center (ABC) he helped launch in Rochester.

But Zubay, then president of ABC, was not alone in helping launch the successful organization. It's inaugural project was a contract from Leroy Shane to manufacture for them 50,000 tom-tom drums.

Zubay told me, "Shane was fundamental to getting ABC off the ground."

Ken Zubay in 1959.

Shane's novelty shop: its gags, local souvenirs and ephemera

"I ordered no pizza!?" went a confused Steve Martin as Centurion Likus Flavius in the classic Saturday Night Live skit *The Vandals*.

He went on, "I don't understand it! What possible pleasure could someone derive from this?" to which his Lieutenant responded, "They think it's funny, sir."

The Vandals was set in 421 AD not long after actual recorded evidence of the first practical joke in 220 AD. Purportedly, the eccentric Roman emperor Elagabalus fashioned leather air-pillows on which unsuspecting guests would sit and thus begat the *Whoopie Cushion*.[12]

Why is this important?

Humor has a way of creating joy and disarming dire conditions.

Consider this excerpt from a 1932 essay, published deep in the throes of the Great Depression, from the *Mobile Register*:

---

[12] Practical joke history goes further back if you are inclined to believe that the aliens who build the pyramids pulled on the Sphinx the ol' "Got your nose" bit.

The yo-yo is back on counters. One hardly dares to shake hands with a friend because of the *joy buzzer* which may lie concealed in his palm.

Surely a nation which can turn to these toys is not a nation bowed down in sorrow. Surely the public mind which can derive amusement and delight from such toys is not a public mind that is distressed to distraction by stock-market reports or weighed down by the weekly and voluminous findings of finance committees.

The capacity for enjoyment is inversely proportionate to the capacity for sorrow. Therefore we may accept the cause of our national distress as purely trivial since such trivial toys as are mentioned here have the ability to raise us to a point of hysterical amusement.

The world is made safer, if not saner, by yo-yos, trick matchboxes and joy-buzzers.

Avaunt then unavailing fears. Away the mists of terror and the lightnings of dismay. The joy-buzzer, the yo-yo and the trick matchbox dispel them. A guffawing populace, delighted at the success

---

Samuel S. Adams received a patent for his *Joy Buzzer* in 1932 which immediately took the depressed country by storm.

The April 11, 1932 *Asbury Park Press* reported that the local manufacturer's novelty found a fan base among these then-celebrities:

New York Governor Alfred E Smith.

Famously flamboyant New York City Mayor and frequenter of "upper class speakeasies" Jimmy Walker.

Actor Maurice Chevalier.

Heavyweight boxing champion Max Schmeling.

Uber-popular radio commentator, newspaper columnist and opinion-setter Walter Winchell.

Shocking.

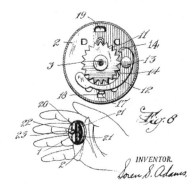

INVENTOR.
Loren S. Adams

Illustration from Adams' 1931 patent filing.

of their little plots to deceive with tricks and gadgets is not a populace to inspire fear nor to menace with a darkling brow the safety of this civilization.

Of course, the Great Depression had ended by the time that Leroy Shane came to the *Med City*[13] for a check-up. But that which buoyed spirits in the 1930s was timeless and even a decade after the introduction of the *Joy Buzzer*, Shane observed on his arrival in 1943 that Rochester was a city in desperate need of distraction. Distraction not from the harsh winter climate, but from the often times grim diagnoses that hung like dark clouds over its many visitors. That he, a one-time broom salesman, could dispense some of the best medicine, laughter — well, he had found his calling.

Gags were but one of the mainstays of Shane's *The Shepherd of the Sand Hills* souvenir store on SE 2nd Street in downtown Rochester but perhaps for which he was best known.

> Rochester Souvenirs—
> ## Jokes - Tricks - Magic
> Gifts for the Family or a Sick Friend
> Gifts for Fun and Parties
> Genuine Indian Handcraft
> Browse Around in the Only Store of
> Its Kind in the Northwest
> Retail and Wholesale
>
> ## LE ROY SHANE
> "Shepherd of the Sand Hills"
> 7-11 S E 2d St.—Just off Broadway
> 2 doors west of Great Western Depot

"The only store of its kind in the Northwest." An advertisement for Leroy Shane's novelty shop from the 1946 Rochester City Directory.

One attendee at a Charter House presentation I delivered several years ago fondly reminisced, "when you needed fake vomit you went to Shane's."

And Shane didn't just sell the novelty items, he was probably the shop's best customer as Michael's restaurateur Charlie Pappas and long-time Shane salesman Ray Raver recounted. Evidently Shane would frequently go about town with one or more of the gags ready to ply then against any of the city's unsuspecting business leaders.

---

[13] Rochester, Minnesota. So-called because of the famous Mayo Clinic that calls it home.

231 RAZZ CUSHION

Heavy weight imported Razz Cushion. Party sensation.

$2.40 Doz.

396 DOGONNIT NOVELTY. This is the well known Joke that is blamed on the Dog. Now better than ever in the new Style. **$3.00 Doz.**

220
JOY BUZZER
Simple hand shake will startle your friends, easily concealed.
$3.60 doz.

Leroy Shane was a purveyor of the trifecta of venerable gag pranks. From top left, The Whoopee Cushion (Shane's 1957), Fake dog-doo (1957), the Joy Buzzer (1950).

But Shane's shop went beyond practical jokes.

"Vacationers buy souvenirs," columnist Harold Severson wrote in a 1957 *Post-Bulletin* profile of Leroy Shane, "and pennants and postcards."

"Greeting cards" like these could be purchased from Shane's *Shepherd of the Sand Hills* shop. (Left and Right from the author's collection.)

In addition to wholesaling these souvenirs across six states, Shane retailed a great many in his shop, some specifically for visitors to the Mayo Clinic.

Some of the most popular vacation memories are these: postcards. Shane's line included scenes from prominent Rochester buildings, usually the Mayo Clinic. (From the author's collection.)

Above and across: Several advertisements from 1948 and 1949 issues of *Know* magazine for Rochester visitors. Left to right: "Shane himself" and a bold statement, "World's Largest Souvenir Store (did anyone tell Wall Drugs?); the Magic House because tricks make for some of the best gags.

Genuine Indian handcrafts like Shane's line of *Big Chief Tom-Toms* were some of Shane's biggest sellers. Shane's successor would later have problems with the claim. The *Mystic Order of the Itching Stitch* was but one of the Mayo Clinic-related souvenirs visitors could take home with them.

Shane's "Shepherd of the Sandhills" storefront on Rochester's North side of 2nd Street Southeast, an area today occupied by the DoubleTree Hotel and adjacent 1st Street Parking Ramp.

Souvenir business

En route to New Orleans via the Sangamon River nearly 200 years ago, a self-made spry young man named Abraham Lincoln stopped in New Salem, near Illinois capitol Springfield. There and for a time he called it home, building first a law practice then launching a burgeoning political career as the area's representative in the Illinois General Assembly.

More recently, the town's been frozen in time through a historical reconstruction of life in the 1830s when Lincoln lived there and is a popular tourist destination especially for busloads of Chicago-area children like yours truly who visited the town with my 8th-grade class.

But for a child, this type of history is dry — "Did he get in sword fights?" "Did he operate a guillotine?" — and my cohorts and I found the air-conditioned souvenir shop much more interesting with its shelves overflowing with switchblade combs, gigantic cigars, and a variety of other essentials that had nothing whatsoever to do with the legacy of the Great Emancipator. (The alligator pencil was particularly popular though in retrospect I do not understand why.)

My budget accommodated a small cedar treasure box, a pleasant-smelling little container for my dimes and paper clips. I had enough cash left over for a totally useless but otherwise necessary corncob pipe which was a best seller solely

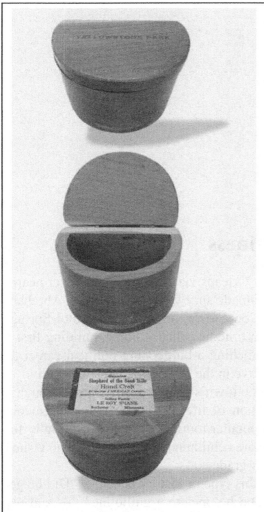

A *distinctive AMERICAN creation*. A Yellowstone Park 4-inch cedar souvenir box manufactured by Leroy Shane. (From the author's collection.)

on account of its price and the unwritten requirement that we return home with as little possible spending money our parents gave us.

Leroy Shane supplied novelty stores across the Midwest and upper Midwest with items like those and it was a large part of his empire.

"What are vacations made of," Harold Severson wrote in a 1957 *Rochester Post-Bulletin* profile. "Besides eating, viewing the scenery and dreaming of home, vacationers buy souvenirs. They spend generously on pennants, pillows, tee shirts or Indian dolls. And plaques, comic ash trays and salt and pepper sets, too."

"It's a highly-competitive business," VP and GM Phil Sternberg added in that profile. "We've restricted ourselves to a six-state area and the major resorts in famed vacation places."

Those places included Yellowstone National Park, Niagara Falls, Mount Rushmore and a souvenir shop owned by Buffalo Bill's grandson.

With so many souvenir shops across so many miles, how did the Shepherd of the Sand Hills know how best to leverage his sales resources?

Longtime Leroy Shane salesman Ray Raver who travelled with Shane on many of those sales calls said, "Shane opened this large copy of Dun & Bradstreet that he traveled with and circled the names of the largest most successful businesses in the town they were next approaching."

No. 817/69 – JUMBO CIGARS–OZARK BOX
No. 817/50 – JUMBO CIGARS–GRT.
SMOKY MTN. BOX.
Per Box $3.75

Popular souvenir store items included giant cigars (above) and corncob pipes (below) which rarely had anything to do with the legacy of the site on which the shop operated. (From an undated Fairway Catalog.)

No. 2328 – MINIATURE COB PIPES.
Rough finish, plastic bits. 6 doz. to box minimum.
Per Dozen. $3.00

Shane fun fact

In the classic 1955 *Honeymooners* episode, *'Twas the Night Before Christmas*, Ralph and Ed are having an exchange about the Japanese novelty box Ralph is gifting Alice.

Ralph says, "The guy [who sold it to me] told me that this is the only one of these in the whole world, that at one time, this was in the house of the Emperor of Japan. It was smuggled into this country ... I just can't wait to see the expression on her face when she gets this."

Ed replies, "I'd like to see the expression on the Emperor of Japan's face when he finds out it's missing!"

It's hysterical, to be sure, but imagine in context, Japanese novelty boxes as cheesy gifts was actually a thing as noted below in Shane's 1950 catalog:

JAPANESE NOVELTY BOXES
Souvenired with Gold Leaf Imprint of Your Locality in any reasonable quantity.

1644—MYSTERY BOX	1627–BIRD CIGARETTE BOX	1626—MYSTIC BOX	1629—DOG CIGARETTE DISPENSER
Secret method necessary. Five distinct moves will open it. Novel Cigarette Box. **$7.20 Doz**	Looks like Juke Box. Open top and bird goes down, picking up a cigarette in its bill. Holds full pack. **$16.50 Doz**	Secret catch holds mystery. Vital spot well concealed. Find it and watch box spring open like magic. Novel cigarette box. **$5.40 Doz**	Well painted box. Holds full pack of cigarettes. Pull top back and moving arms lift cigarette right up to dogs mouth. **$7.20 Doz**
1639—SECRET PANEL BOX Identical construction as above, with sliding panel.... **$7.20 Doz**	1638—FLAT TRICK BOX Small cigarette box with secret sliding panel. **$3.00 Doz**		

Leroy Shane, Inc.

Leroy Shane, Incorporated, that is, Shane's wholesale catalog business, began life Wednesday September 1, 1948 as the "Fun of the Month Club, Inc.," five years after Shane arrived in Rochester with a beginning capital of $1,000.00

The names of the "Fun of the Month Club" incorporators and first board of directors are largely familiar: Leroy Shane (President), Phil Sternberg (Vice-President and General Manager) and Mabel Evenson (Secretary, Treasurer and Office Manager). A forth officer, however, is something of a mystery: Bojas Oksner.

In 1945, Oksner, a World War I veteran, had been a manager at Ralph H. Miller's ladies apparel shop, while his wife was a clerk for Leroy Shane. Little else is known of him other than that he must have played a significant role in Shane's early days based on this prominent entry from the 1948 Rochester City Directory:

SHANE, LE ROY (LeRoy Shane), r 201 Castelamar Apts.
SHANE, LE ROY (LeRoy Shane and Bojas Oksner), Wholesaler and Retailer; Hand Craft Novelties, Shepard of the Hills, Unique Wood Carvings, Genuine Indian Craft, Novelty and Art Ware, 7 2d S E, tel 2-2006. (See card under Novelties—Wholesale and Retail).

On January 27, 1950, the "Fun of the Month Club" incorporation saw two significant amendments: the corporation

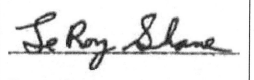

Though Shane's organization was often called simply "Leroy Shane," he signed his name uniquely.

name was changed from *Fun of the Month Club, Inc.,* to *Leroy Shane, Inc.,* and for the first time, officers were named: Philip Sternberg, President (!) and Le Roy Shane, Secretary.

Shane's souvenir and catalog concern did well but was not the only such operation in country. In 1952, Eugene Fishgoll bought a small souvenir shop that was centered in the Ozarks and expanded it to the Fairway Manufacturing Company which is still today operating in St. Louis, Missouri.

At first both were symbiotic, Fairway President Mark Sobelman, grandson of founder Fishgoll, said. Shane provided its popular drum line to Fairway and Fairway supplied various Chinese-made items like ceramic plates and plush animals to Shane's customers.

But by the early 60s, Shane's souvenir business was floundering. Evidently, Mark Sobelman recalled, Shane had sold his equity in *Leroy Shane, Inc.* to finance his Diets of Rochester effort, his goal being that of a big player in the emerging TV dinner space but was under-capitalized and a decade before his time.

On September 25, 1961, the Fairway Manufacturing Company merged with, but in practicality *acquired*, Leroy Shane, Inc.

At the time of the merger, Fairway's Eugene and wife Lillian Fishgoll were the majority Shane shareholders owning about 37.5% of the Rochester-based company. Philip Sternberg maintained the next-largest stake holding about 25% of the business. Other owners of *Leroy Shane, Inc.* were Herbert Sobelman who was Fishgoll's son and current President Mark Sobelman's father, and Albert Levinson who was Fishgoll's brother-in-law. Neither Bojas Oksner nor Mabel Evenson maintained any capital at the time of the merger.

Fairway kept Sternberg on largely to maintain continuity with existing Shane customers and otherwise left the Rochester facility to operate independently.

However, the devastating Rochester 1978 flood and a subsequent explosion wiped-out the Silver Lake-based building and when things resumed locally, Fairway took over operations.

September 1, 1948 Minnesota incorporation of the *Fun of the Month Club, Inc.* Where it all started.

A gust of wind caught this trailer and flipped it and the car upside
down. Phil Sternberg and salesman John Kirlin were injured.
The car and trailer were total losses while, "several thousand dollars worth of souvenirs and novelty items inside the trailer were
damaged." (Photo copyright 1974 *Winona Daily News*. Used with
permission.)

Shane contemporaries

Phil Sternberg

"When [World War II] had ended," *Rochester Post-Bulletin's* Harold Severson wrote, "Phil Sternberg, native of Rochester who had been involved in his earlier years in the hotel, restaurant, and clothing business, returned from service. He teamed-up with Shane in developing the manufacturing end of the business."

But Severson left out a lot, a whole lot.

If company name-sake Leroy Shane was the heart of Leroy Shane, Inc. — the "idea guy" who fancied himself, as one contemporary called him, *a mover and shaker* — Sternberg was the legs who, though holding several executive titles, was perhaps best deserving of General Manager.

General Manager Phil Sternberg in his office. Photo from the 1957 Leroy Shane catalog.

Phil Sternberg in 1957 with some of the items Shane distributed for the Prairie Island Dakota and other similarly-themed goods under their subsidy *Indian Traders*. Photo © 1957 Rochester Post-Bulletin. Used with permission.

By many accounts, Sternberg ran the operation.

No conversation I had about Leroy Shane didn't include a sidebar involving Sternberg.

Sternberg had been with Shane from the very beginning and it was his name on press releases as far back as 1948 advertising the *Fun of the Month Club* with, "If you're looking for fun, we're looking for you."

And it was Sternberg who shepherded through the merger with St. Louis, Missouri's Fairway Manufacturing and stayed-on to run the Rochester operations through the early 1980s after Shane had retired. Sternberg also managed the Fairway/Shane-owned *Avenue Gifts and Gadgets Shop* in the Kahler Hotel.

Phil Sternberg died on March 19, 2001 in Rochester, Minnesota at the age of 91.

Walt Bruzek

"Organized by a Screwball — maintained for fun."

That was the original motto of Walt Bruzek's "Bear Fax Club," whose founding members were those readers of his similarly named Owatonna, Minnesota newspaper column.

In 1968 his club reorganized and held formal events in what was then called the *Clinic City* towards fellowship and to provide revenue to its "worthwhile fund" which provided financing for area projects like a renovation at the Olmsted County Historical Society.

In addition to Southeast Minnesota booster and columnist, Bruzek was an Owatonna city councilman, an avid sports historian, a KROC radio personality, and an amateur magician. He was a cofounder of the then-popular Downtown Quarterbacks Club that met frequently at the legendary Michael's Restaurant in downtown Rochester, Minnesota.

But the *raison d'être* for the Old Bear's mention here: Bruzek owned a novelty shop, *The Bear's Den*, in Owatonna and was good friends with Leroy Shane.

Longtime Shane salesman Ray Raver recalled the two were often found joking, or rather, *practical* joking with each

Walt Bruzek at his first annual Bear Fax Club event at the Kahler Hotel in Rochester on January 26, 1971. Inset: with baseball great and frequent Rochester visitor Joe Garagiola. Photo source unknown.

other and a 1945 *Albert Lea Evening Tribune* immortalized one such incident. This, during the time the U. S. mint briefly substituted steel for copper during a war shortage of the latter. While popular today with coin collectors, merchants then lamented their similarity to dimes.

Helped take "Steel" pennies out of circulation

Rochester. When novelty shop proprietors get together, pennies change hands. Walter Bruzek, operator of the Bear's Den novelty shop in Owatonna, didn't like the dime-size silver pennies any better than the rest of us, and proceeded methodically to remove several of them from circulation by accumulating them. Recently he paid a debt to the Shane Gift Shop here with 70 pounds of the unpopular coins — 10,800, worth $108. Question is, what will LeRoy Shane do with them?

Walt Bruzek died in Rochester on December 31, 1981.

Bojas and Bertha Oksner. Little is known of the couple except that Bertha was a clerk for Shane prior to Bojas becoming a partner. (Photo courtesy of Dorothy Oksner.)

Bojas Oksner

Little is known of Bojas Oksner (left) with regards to his days in Rochester, Minnesota. Oksner, just before partnering with Leroy Shane, worked at Ralph H. Miller's ladies apparel shop and at the time his wife, Bertha, worked for Shane.

Not long afterwards, Oksner left Rochester and eventually settled in California.

Oksner died on November 1, 1998. He was 101 years old.

Mystic 13

There is evidently a symbiotic relationship between pur-veyors of novelties and the local community of magicians. In his aforementioned book, *Oh Really, Riley*, longtime proprietor of the legendary Chicago-area gag shop bearing his father's name, Jim Riley discusses his family's *bona fides* as amateur magicians and their shop as a gathering place for area professional magicians.

Similarly, Leroy Shane found himself frequently in the company of like-minded fun fellows, that is to say, practitioners of the legerdemain.

279

CIGARETTE THRU HANDKERCHIEF

Borrow victim's silk handkerchief. Put lighted cigarette right in center of it. Return handkerchief unmarked.   **$1.50 doz.**

One of the tricks Shane wholesaled in his 1950 catalog.

Shane was a member of the area's *Mystic 13* club of magicians and in this circle were the likes of Walt Bruzek who would be frequently seen about town performing his signature rabbit trick and Mayo fellow Ollie Beahrs who was regarded as just as fine a magician as he was a surgeon. Beahrs financed his education by performing magic and years later through his prowess with the scalpel made a portion of President Reagan's prostate disappear.

The *Mystic 13* still exist and one of the current members Brent Coggins, who performs under the name Sin'Gee', shared the photo which appears on the following page depicting the scene backstage after a magic performance at the Mayo Auditorium sometime between 1946 and 1948.

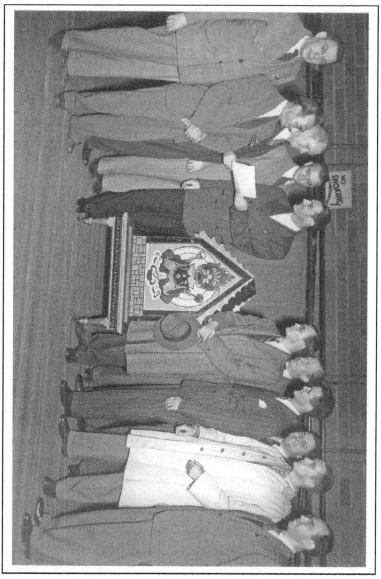

The photo caption reads, "Sternberg had just given a show," but few of the faces are any longer recognizable. The far left gentleman, of course, is LeRoy Shane himself and 3rd from left is Walt Bruzek. Others depicted include Ollie Beahrs and Phil Sternberg. The backside of the photo (next page) is of equal interest as it depicts autographs of all present. Of particular interest is Bruzek's which includes a rabbit doodle as a callback to his signature trick.

Ollie recounted one anecdote of his early years in his autobiography *The Odyssey and Reflections of One Surgeon* that is worthy of sharing here:

During the senior year of [Northwestern University] medical school, the Davises sponsored the *Forties Frolics*, which was the senior class play to be presented as a social event in the Drake Hotel at the time of graduation... My part of the event was to do a special effect that I worked on in my spare time in the carpenter shop in the basement of the medical school building, The effect was to perform an operation. A patient, one of the medical students, was placed on the table and draped, and then after the incision was made, the stomach and other abdominal organs and, finally, a uterus were removed from this male patient. This created an embarrassing situation for the patient; to resolve the issue, the patient and drape were made to float into the air, the drape was lit with a match, and in a puff of smoke the patient disappeared – never to return."

FOR THE MAGIC-MINDED!
FUN OF THE MONTH'S
"TRICK & MAGIC" MEMBERSHIP . . .

How would you like to receive a special kit each month containing 3 or 4 of the latest, most fascinating magic tricks? You can . . . through a FUN OF THE MONTH "Trick & Magic" membership. The fees are the same as a regular FUN OF THE MONTH member-ship. Send coupon today for full information to FUN OF THE MONTH'S "Trick & Magic Department"!

"In the story of Leroy Shane...

...Inc., there is a theme just about as American as Davy Crockett's exploits. Operating under a system of enterprises in which initiative, imagination, determination, perseverance and perspiration bring just rewards, the Rochester firm illustrates how a hope and a dream became a reality; how freedom to make the most of an opportunity can bear fruit; and, how enterprising men — and women — investing time, effort, and capital in business benefit not only themselves but an entire community."

— Rochester Post-Bulletin, June 18, 1955

Index

Other titles from Bamber Books:

A Famous Autograph: The peculations and flight of A K Ward.

Memphis had the blues long before W. C. Handy. In the late 1870s, the city was devastated by a yellow fever epidemic that forced half the population to flee and claimed the lives of a quarter of those who remained. Then another scourge came. His name was Augustus Kenneth Ward. "A Famous Autograph" is the story of A. K. Ward, the nineteenth century's most notorious — and prestigious — forger. He was one of the Memphis elite, earning first their respect with his pedigree (he was the stepson of a Tennessee Governor) then with his shrewd legal and business acumen, their trust. And when the time was right, on an October afternoon in 1895, Ward fled to Central America with the equivalent of seven million dollars and a daughter of the city's most prominent citizen. Ward's peculations and flight were chronicled in newspapers from New York to Honolulu and from Minneapolis to New Orleans. But they didn't tell the whole story: the story of the son of a Civil War casualty raised in privilege; a financial wunderkind who in the span of three years lived in a mansion, a jungle, and a prison; a man who walked the grounds of Graceland decades before Elvis; a man whose notorious signature on rogue financial instruments was coined ... "A Famous Autograph"

H. H. Holmes: A blotch on the White City: Period accounts of Herman W. Mudgett, America's first serial murderer

"God only knows, for I do not, how this man could do such a deed. Devils may know how he could do it, but it is beyond the ken of any human being with a heart to conceive." With those words, the prosecutor summed-up the sentiment of an entire nation aghast at the crimes committed at the so-called "castle" of Herman W. Mudgett, alias H. H. Holmes, during the World's Columbian Exposition in Chicago where the alabaster-colored buildings earned it the moniker "White City." Here is assembled a collection of period accounts to help recreate the excitement and horror of the time; the trial and meted-out justice of America's first serial murderer.

40 Years a Gambler on the Mississippi

"Some men are born rascals. Others have rascality thrust upon them." George H. Devol was an infamous gambler — though "cheat" would be a more accurate word. In his "Forty Years a Gambler on the Mississippi" Devol recounts dozens of anecdotes of how he plied his Three-Card Monte and sharp dealing skills to cheat the cheaters and/or suckers on steamboats and in river towns over more than four decades in the mid-nineteenth-century South.

The Brooklyn Bridge: Its earliest years

"Thousands on thousands will cross the Bridge because it is the Bridge." It's been called the "8th Wonder of the World" and was the object of Ken Burns' first documentary. A fixture in the background of practically every movie or TV show set in New York City, the Brooklyn Bridge stands not just as an urban icon but as testament to engineering, ingenuity, and hard work. "The Brooklyn Bridge: Its Earliest Years" is a collection of 19th century accounts — a broad swath from construction details written by Washington Roebling himself to a souvenir booklet published by a large department store of the day commemorating the bridge's opening; as well as newspaper accounts of early panics and tragedies.

Forty Quarts of Liquor: Fatty Arbuckle and the Death of Virginia Rappe: Hollywood's First Scandal

Nearly a century before Harvey Weinstein and Kevin Spacey shamed Hollywood spawning the #MeToo and Time's-Up movements, popular film star Roscoe "Fatty" Arbuckle — second at the box office only to Charlie

Chaplin — stood trial for the murder of the young starlette Virginia Rappe. Some medical experts, and the court of public opinion, concluded the girl died in a sexual assault after a weekend of consuming illegal alcohol, her bladder having ruptured under Fatty's 266 pounds. But after three trials and a defense that cost Arbuckle more than did O. J. Simpson's "Dream Team," the comedian was freed. The public was never persuaded. "Everywhere today," one period commentary said, "Arbuckle's name, with its unsavory associations, is met with a sneer; everywhere indecent living is branded as 'Fatty Arbuckle stuff.'" Using contemporaneous accounts, "Forty Quarts of Liquor," — a reference to the amount of prohibition-era illegal alcohol Arbuckle's party consumed — documents Hollywood's first scandal.

Leroy Shane: The Shepard of the Sand Hills and the Life of the Party.

He came from Ohio to bring much needed joy to the "Med City," Rochester, Minnesota, home of the world famous Mayo Clinic. But he was much more than a mere 1940's novelty store proprietor. He was a visionary. Shane introduced the first frozen diet dinner, proposed the first gas station mini-mart, and was the first to license the Slinky patent. But more than anything, he was The Shepherd of the Sand Hills and the life of the party.

From de Soto to Elvis: A Brief History of Graceland Farm

Graceland. Heard of it? If you did, that's probably because of its most famous resident, Elvis Presley. But Graceland's history goes back long before 1957 when he purchased the Memphis property. Learn about its first occupant (a forger from Mississippi), its most pampered (a Hereford bull named Rollo Domino), and its days as a hunting ground for the Choctaw and Chickasaw. With illustrations and photos shared with the author by the family of Graceland builder Dr. Thomas D Moore.

Jumbo's Keeper: The autobiography of Matthew Scott and his biography of P.T. Barnum's great elephant Jumbo

Much has been written about the great elephant Jumbo, P.T. Barnum's centerpiece from 1882 until the animal's tragic death in 1885. But what could be more authoritative than that penned here by Jumbo's longtime keeper Matthew Scott? This autobiography of Jumbo's keeper and biography of the most famous pachyderm of all was published in 1885, the same year of that elephant's death. This edition includes Scott's original 1885 book as well as an all-new epilogue that describes Scott's own tragic end. With additional illustrations.

Bamber Books
facebook.com/BamberBooks